CONSTRUCTION VEHICLES COLORING BOOK TODDLERS

THIS BOOK BELONGS TO ......

COLOR TEST PAGES

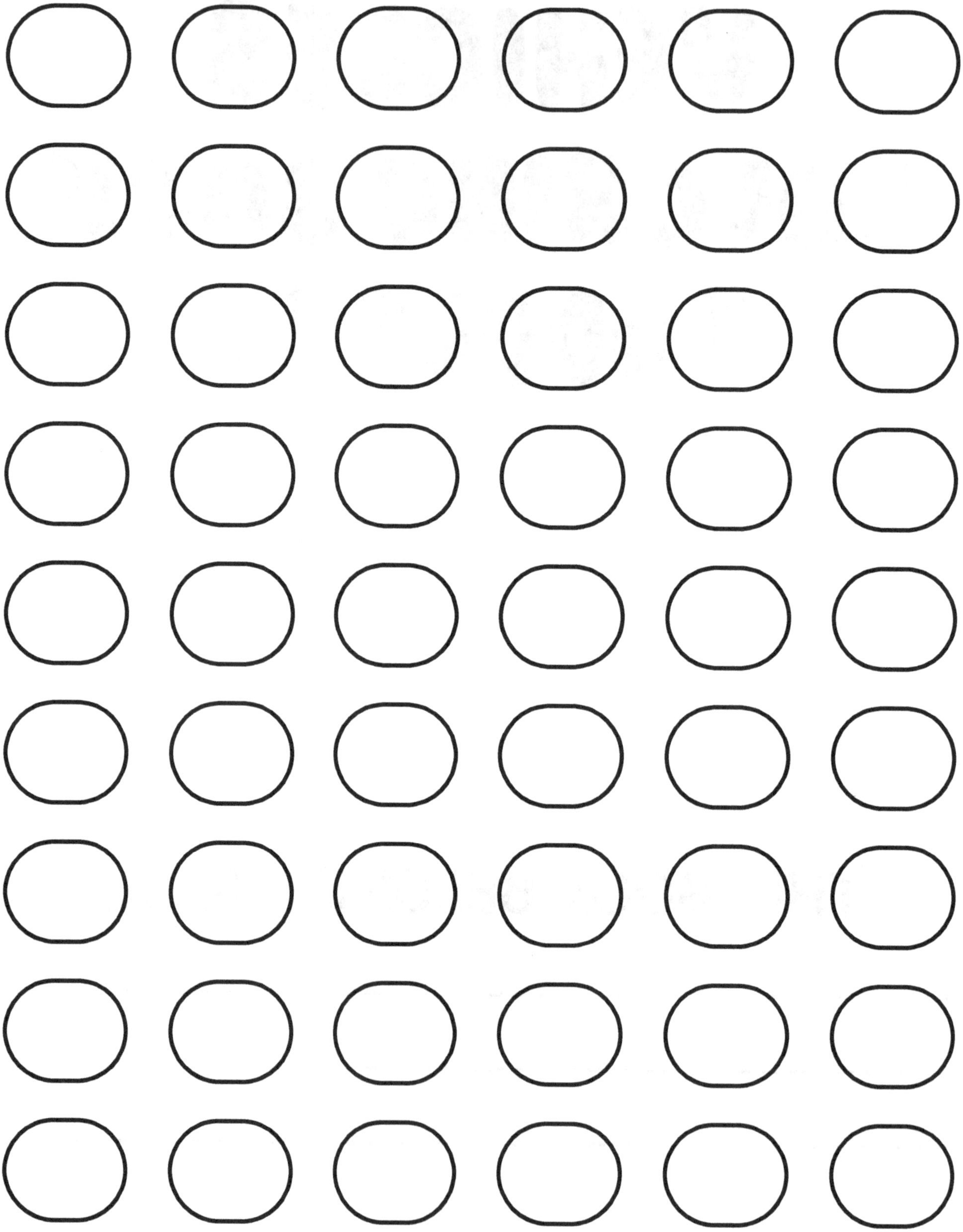

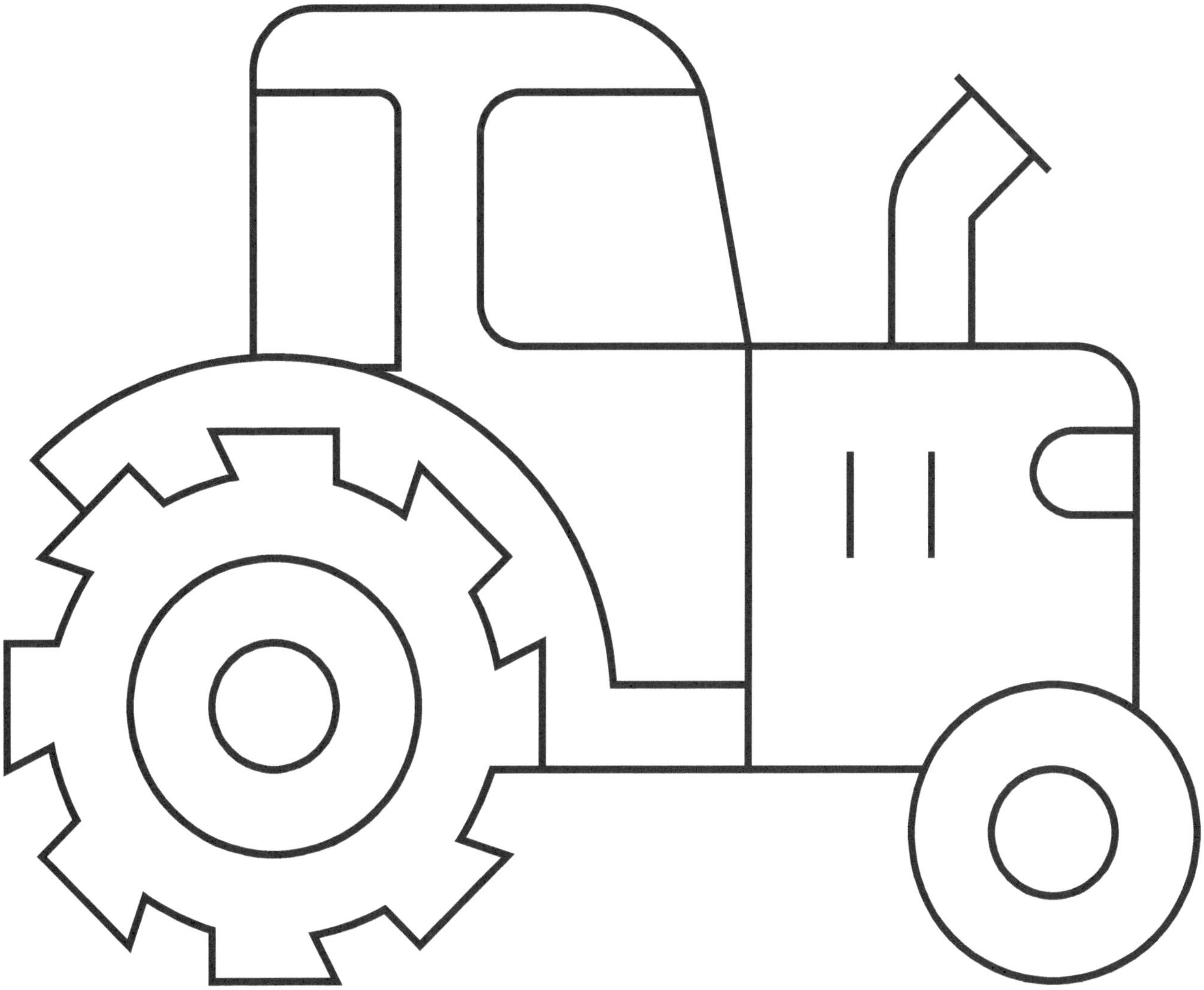

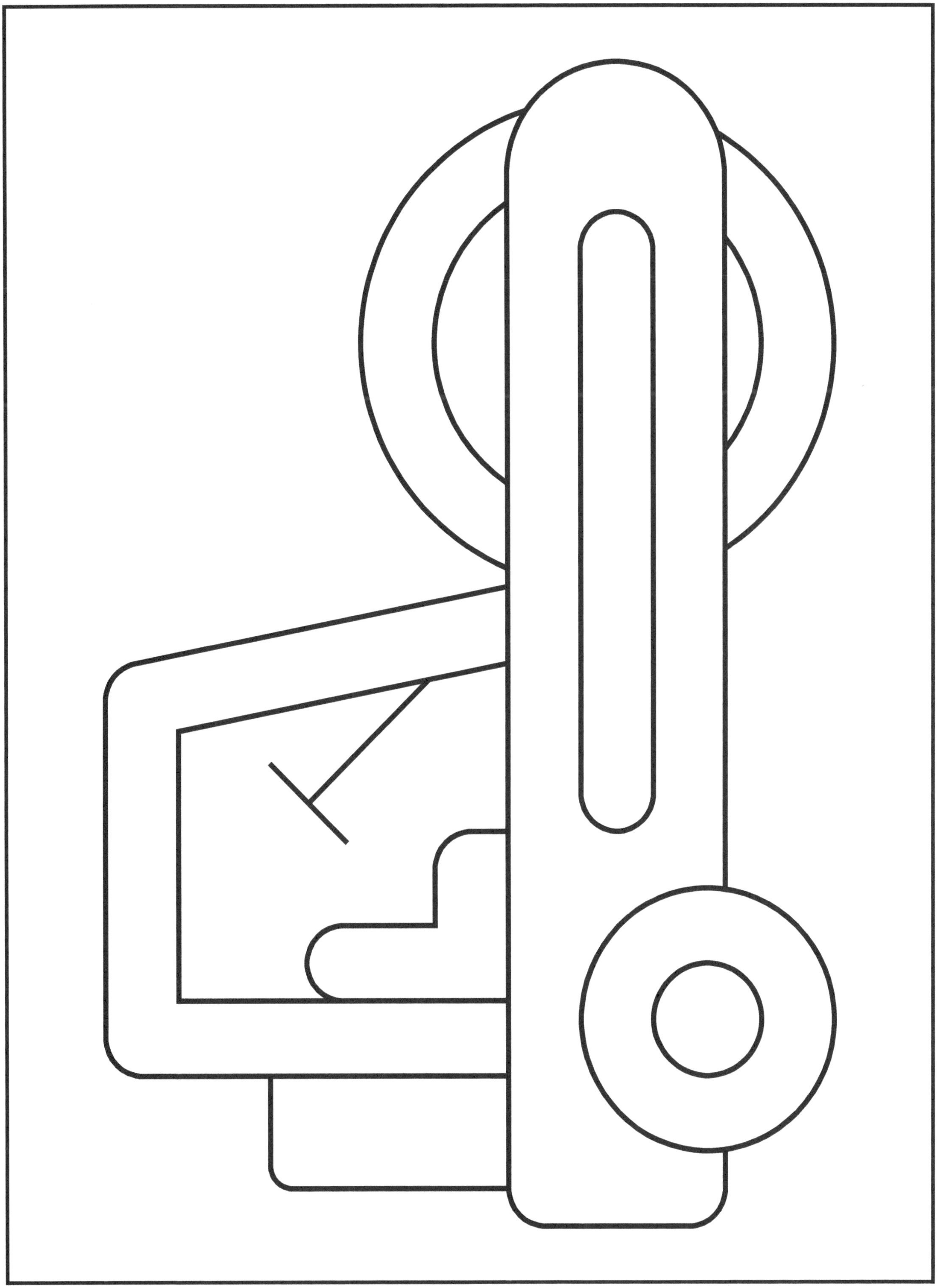

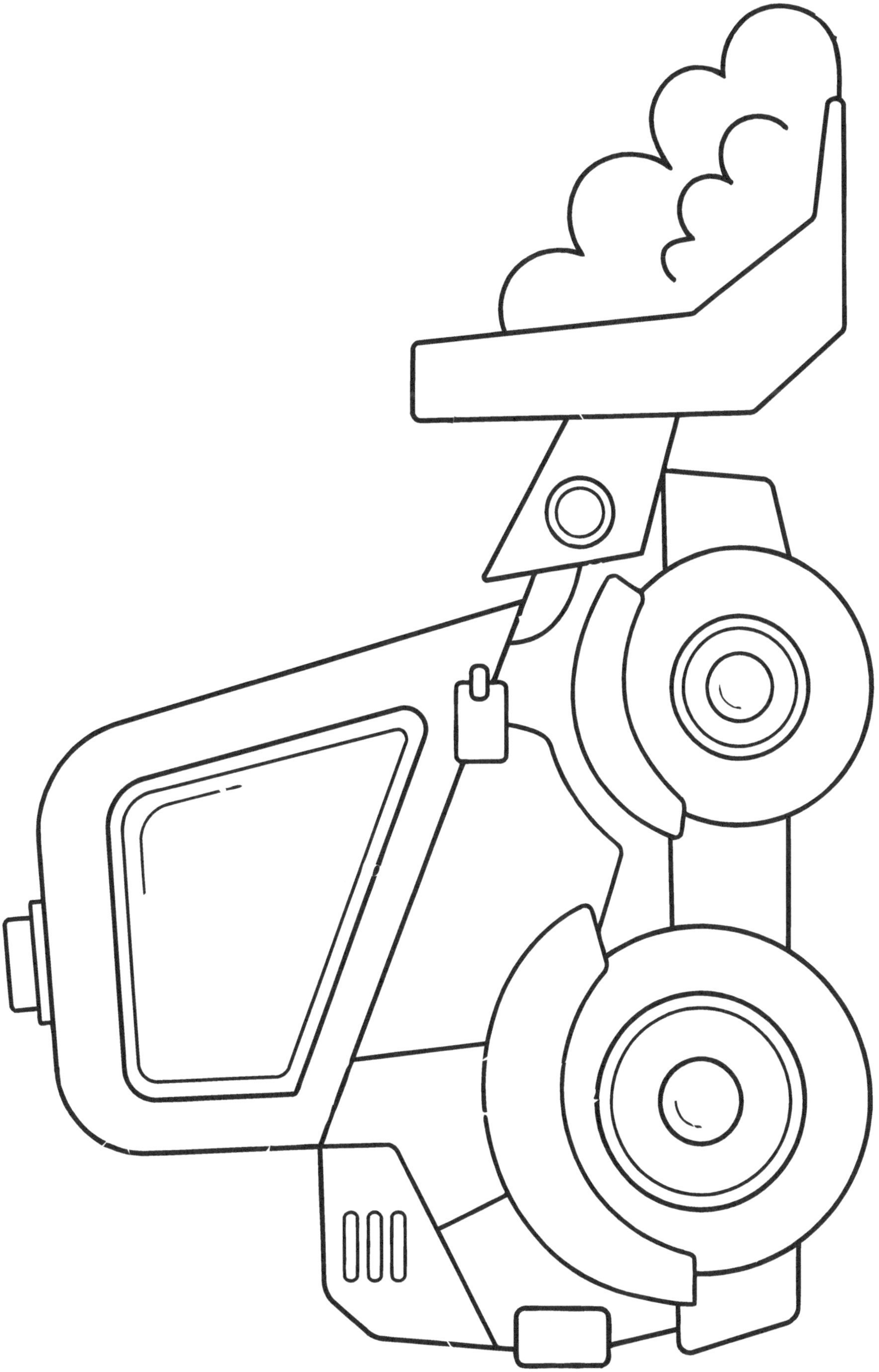

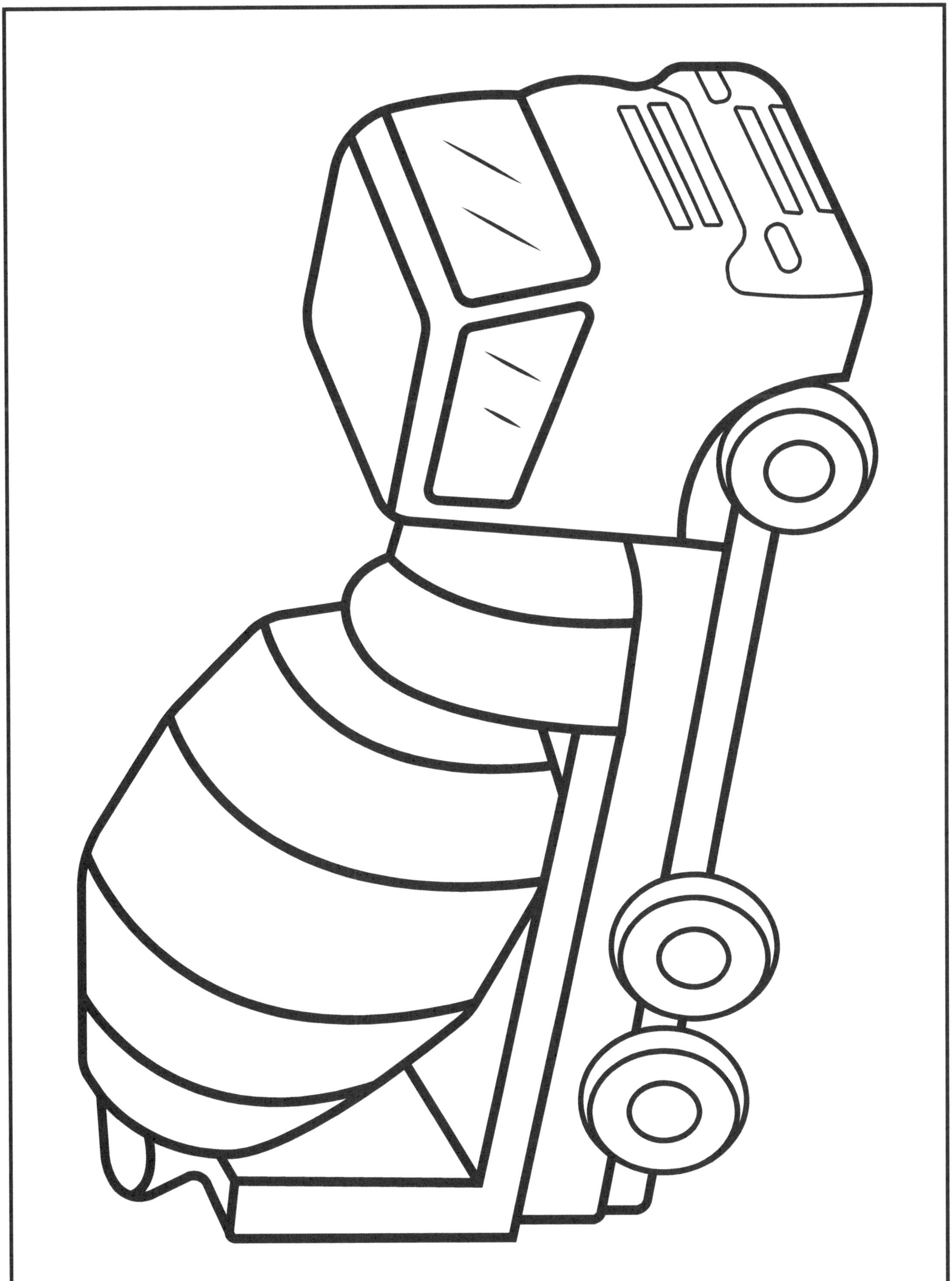

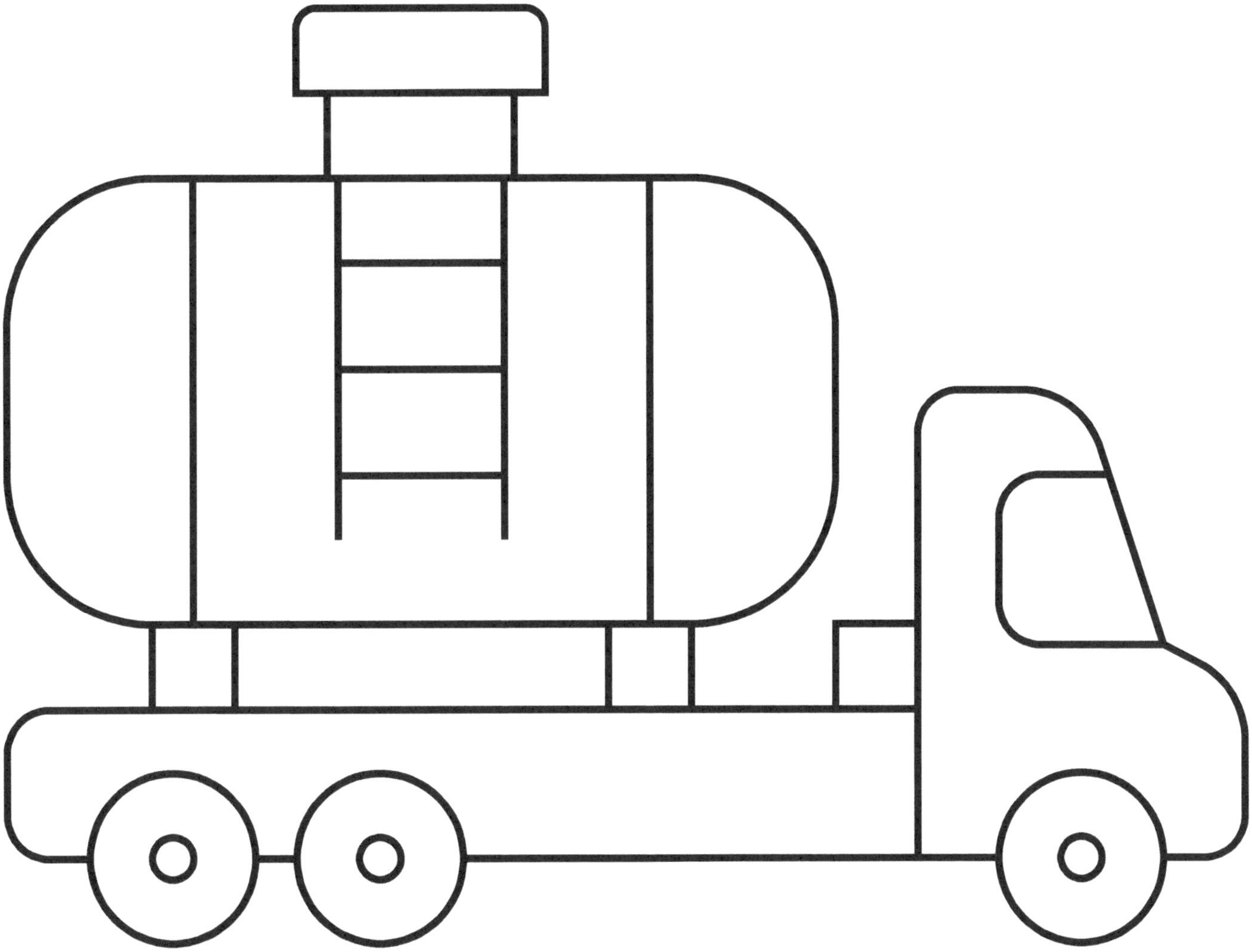

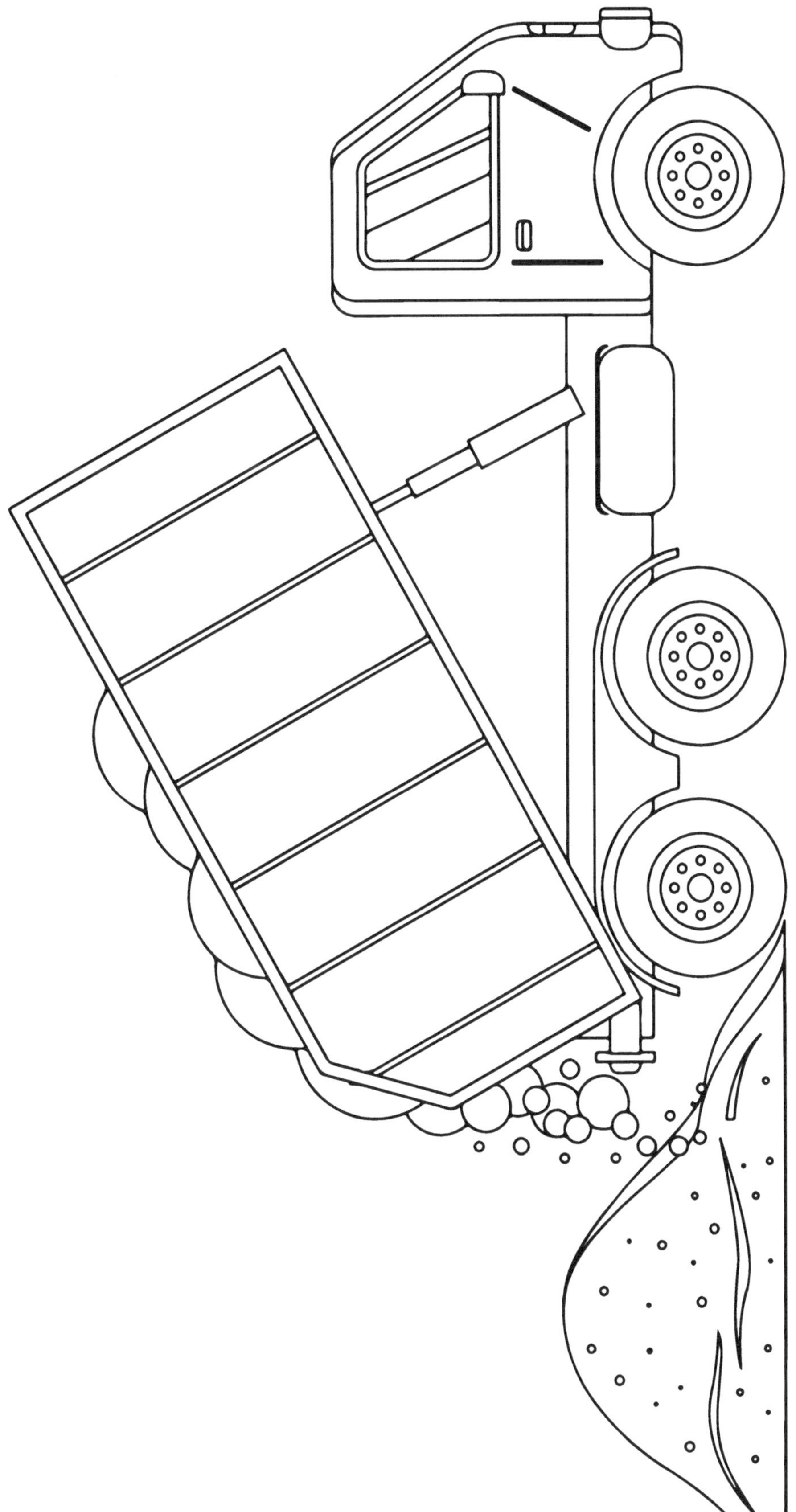

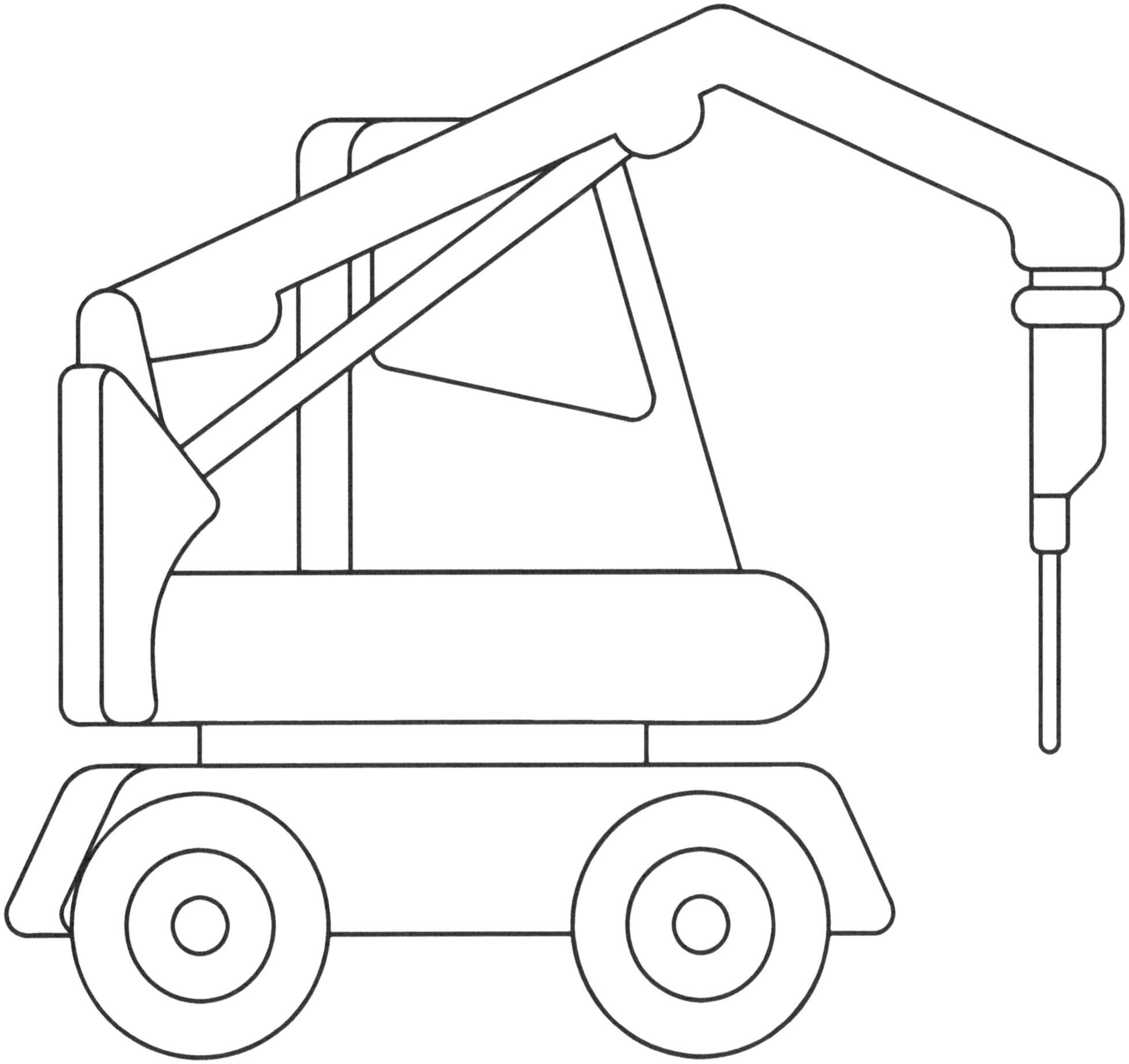

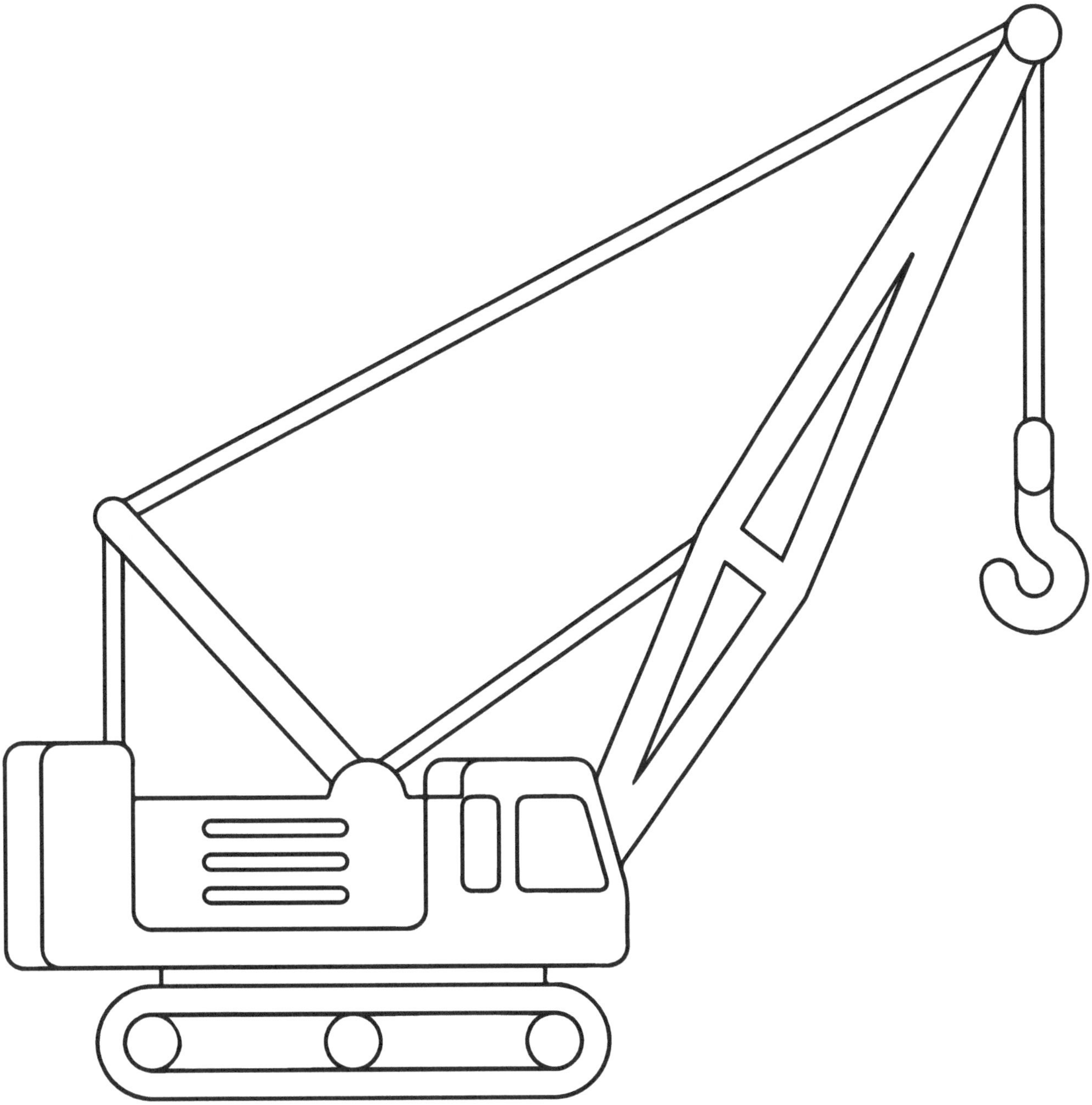

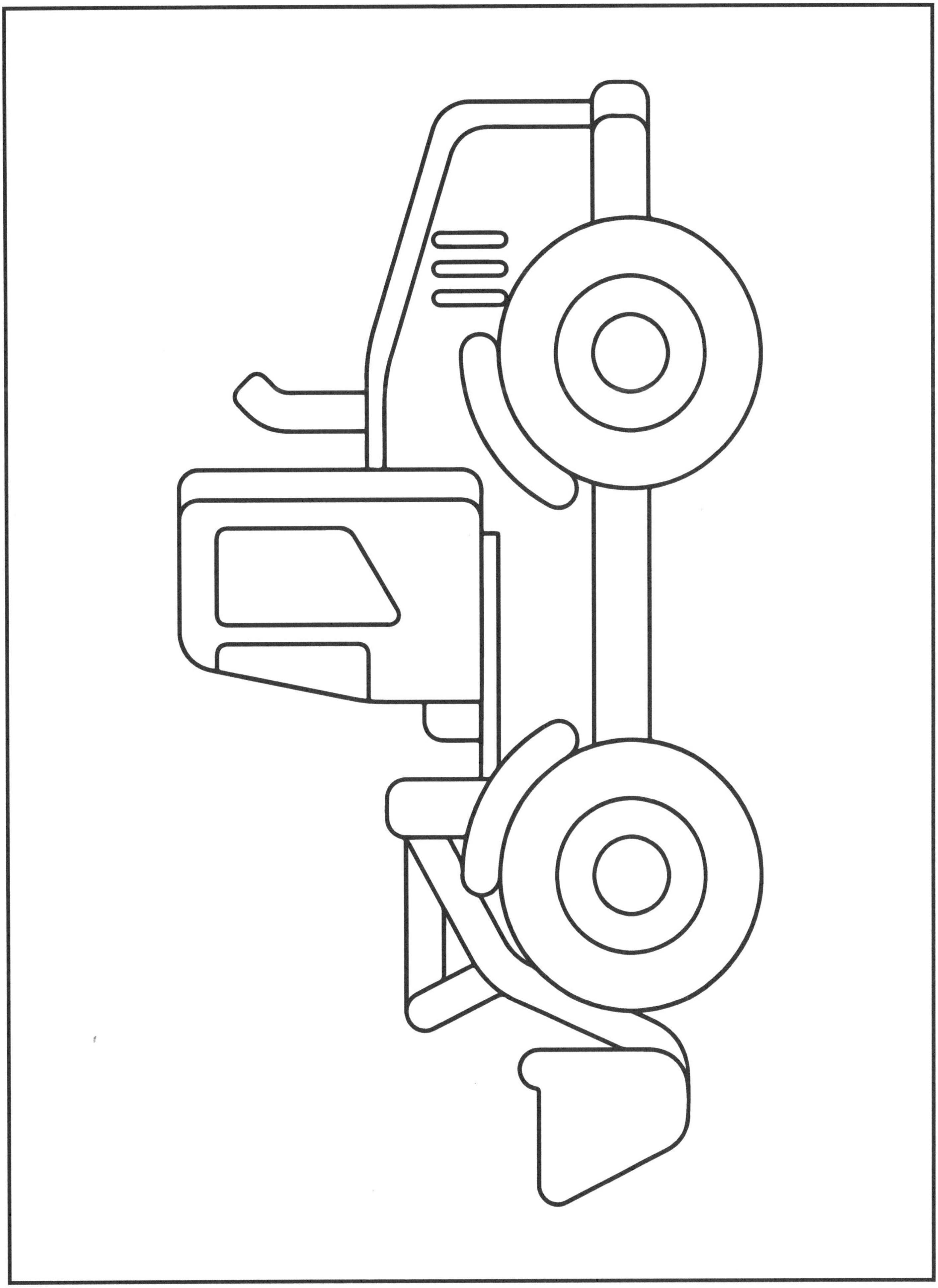

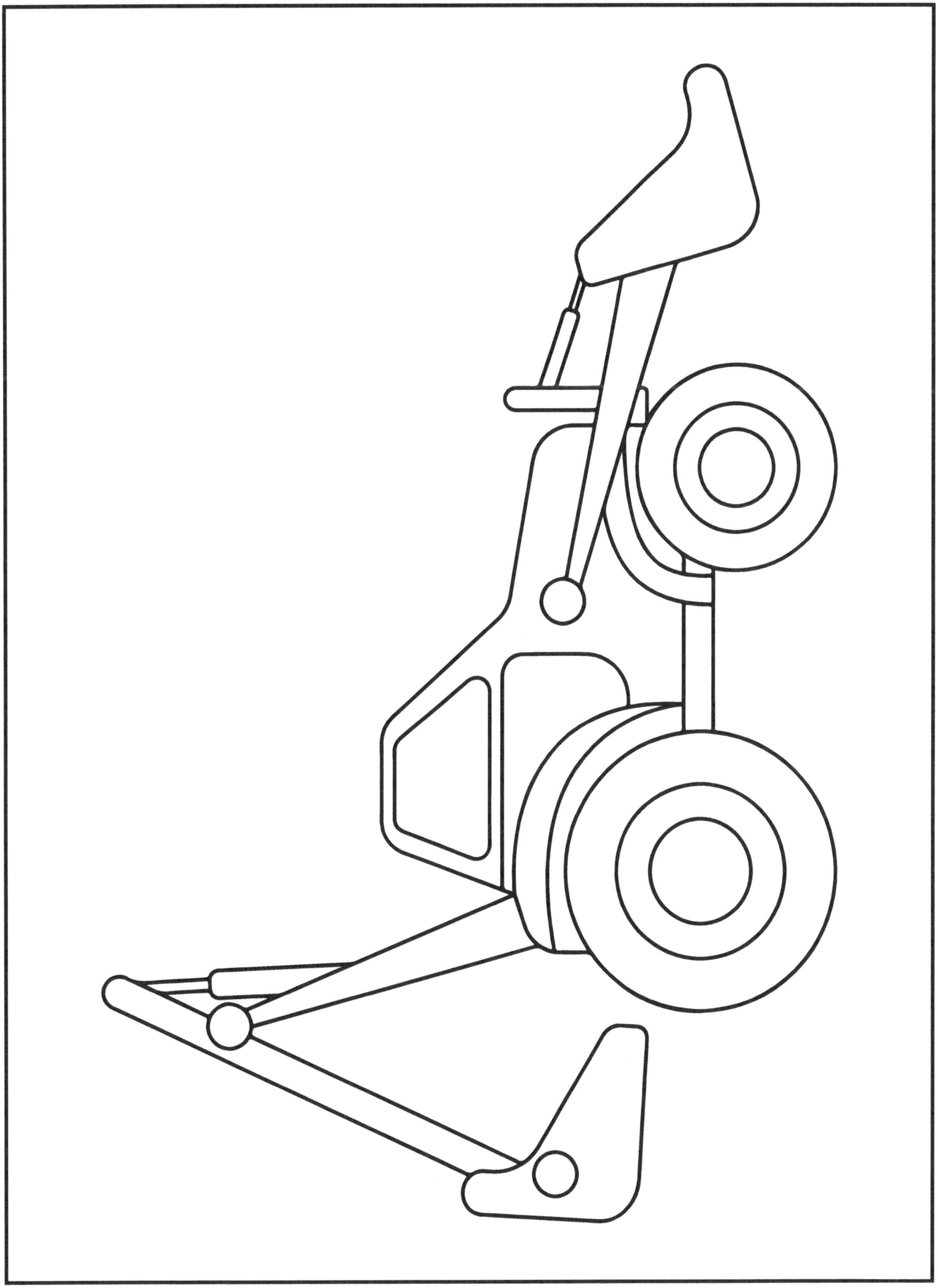

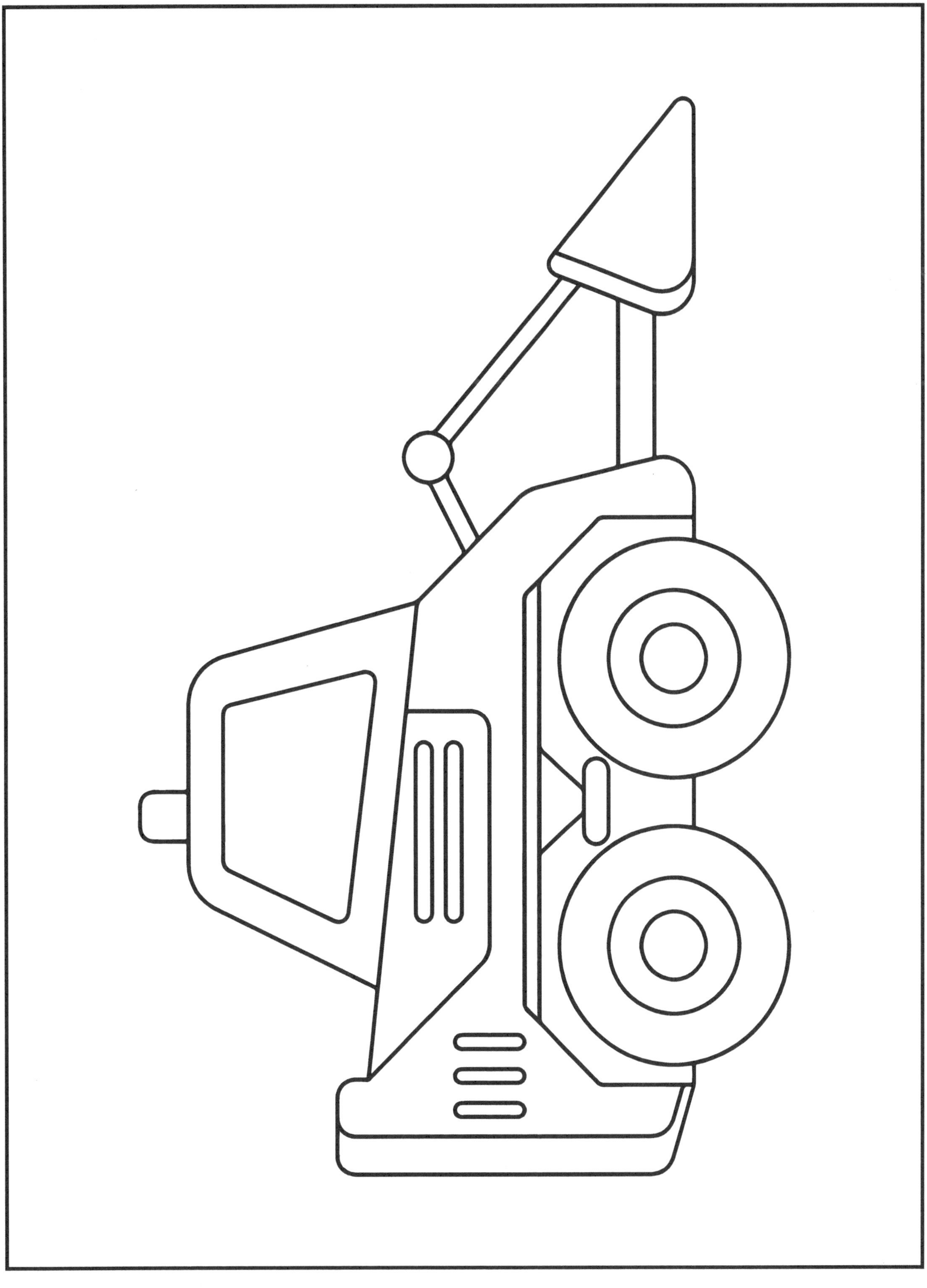

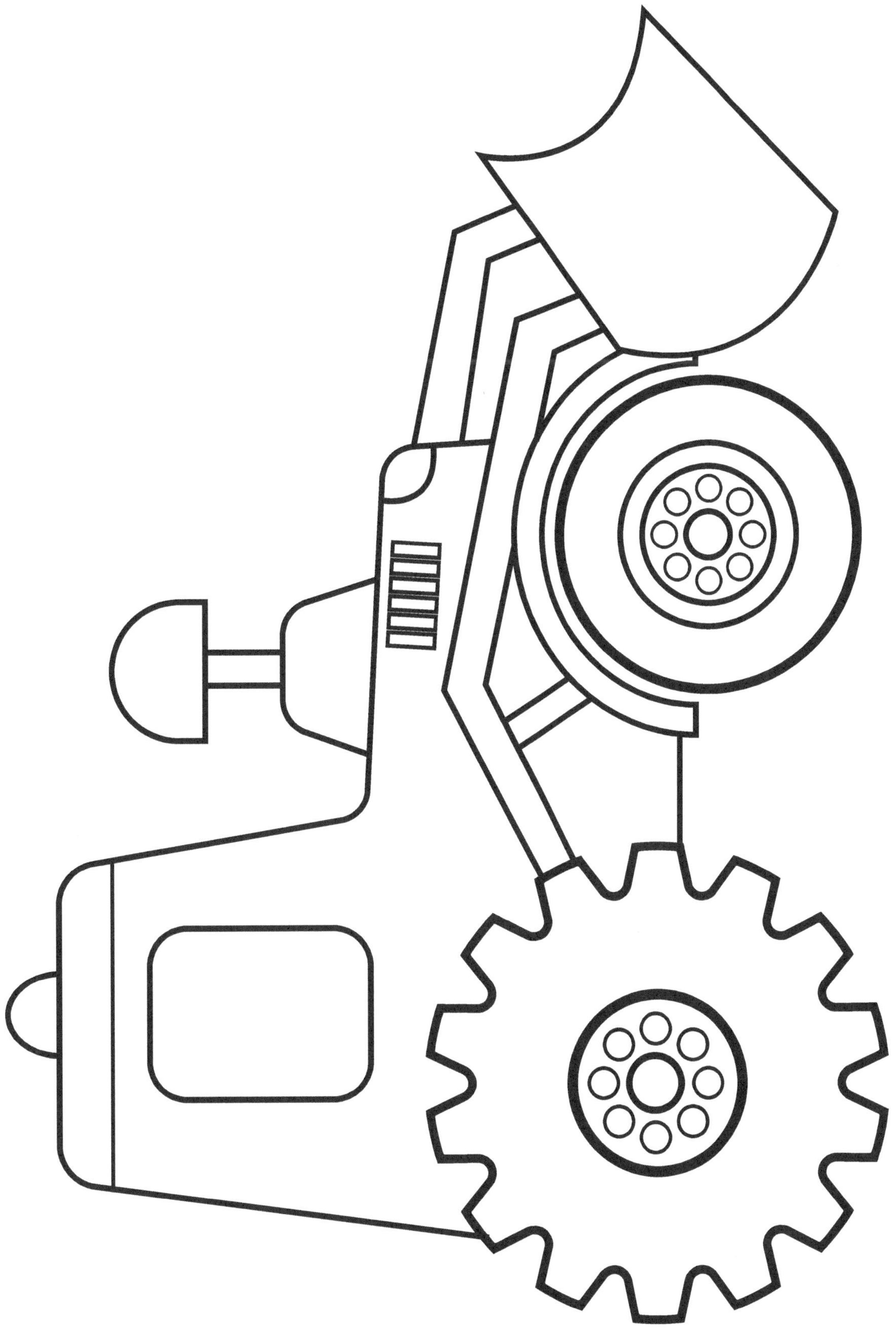

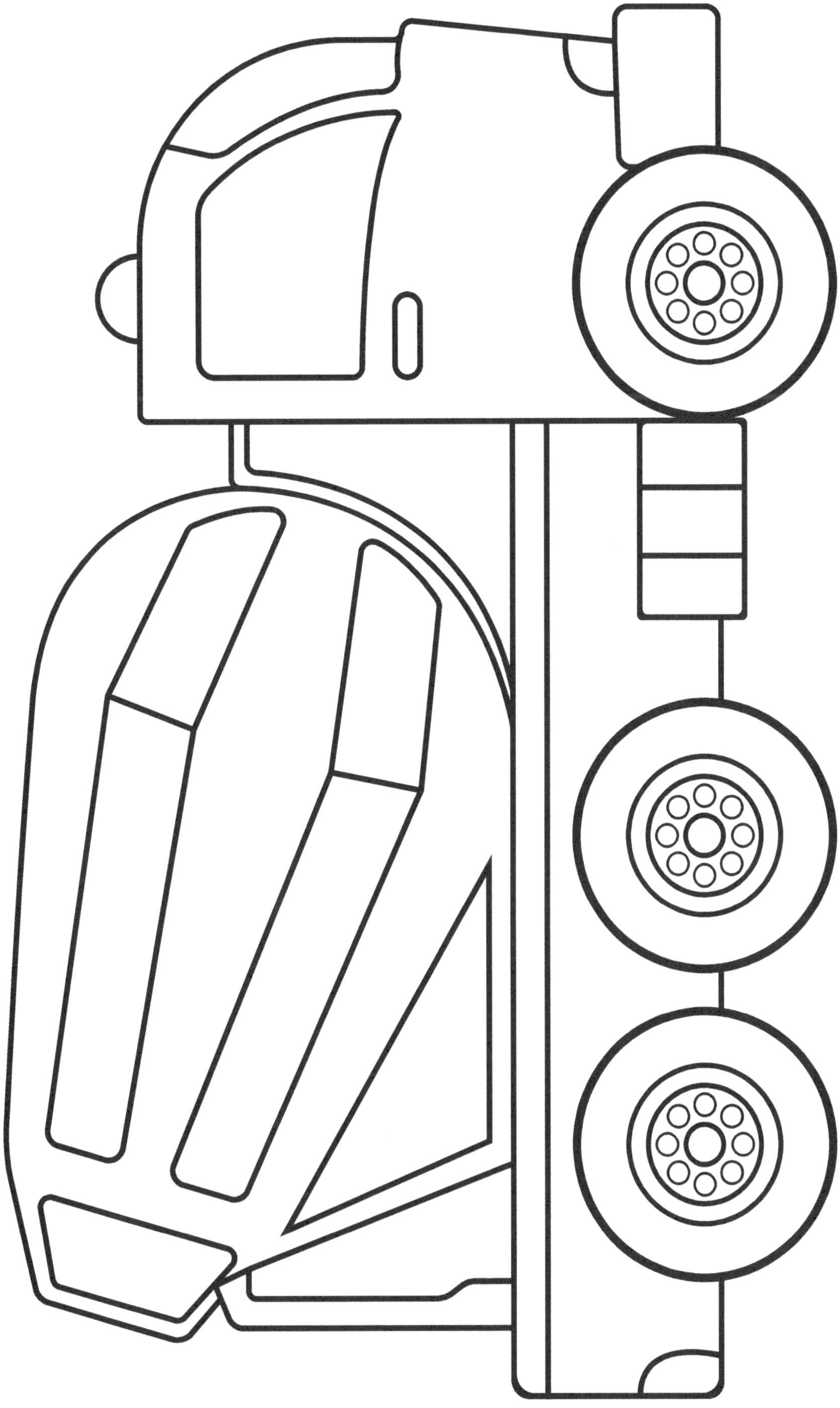

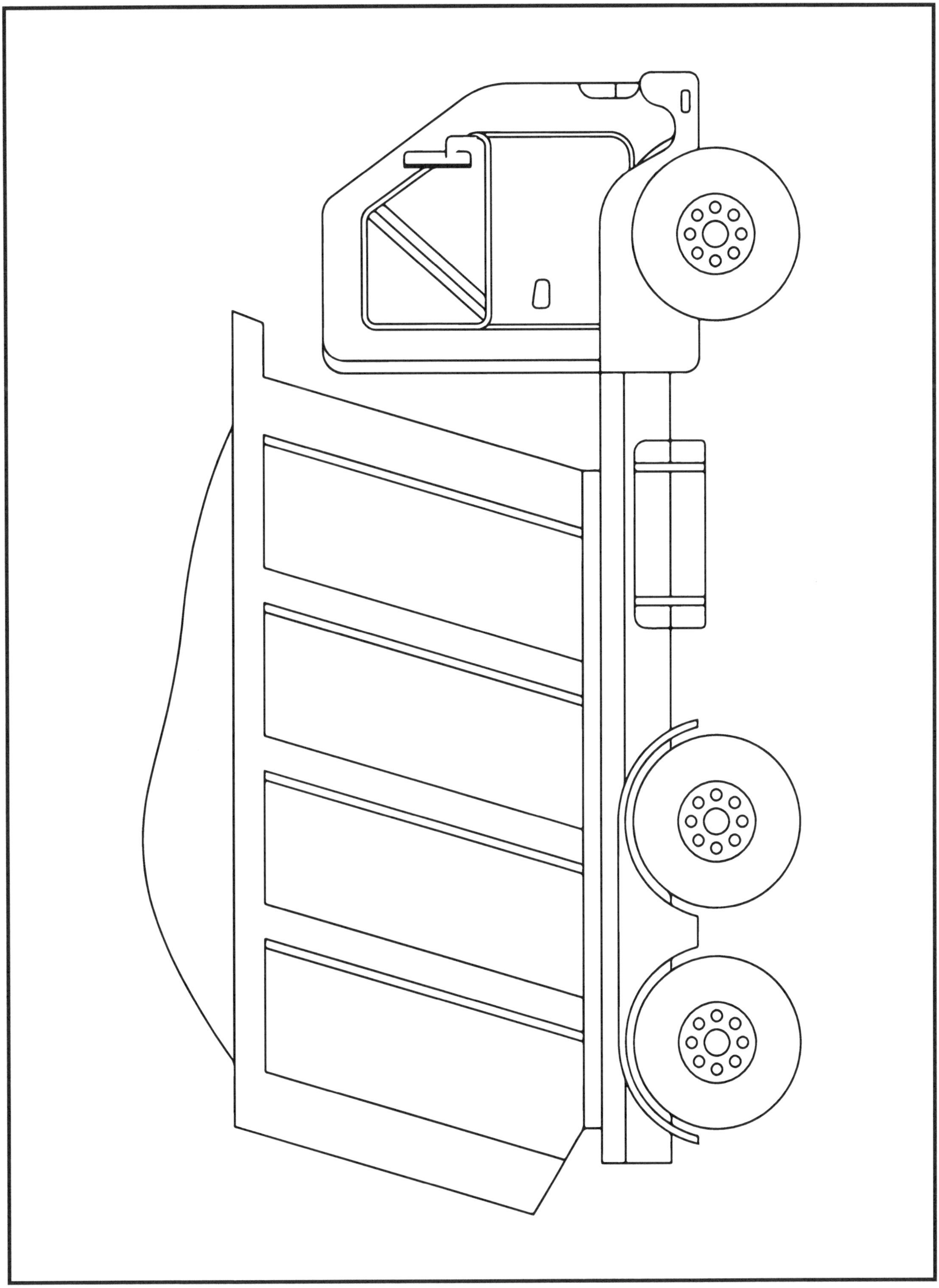

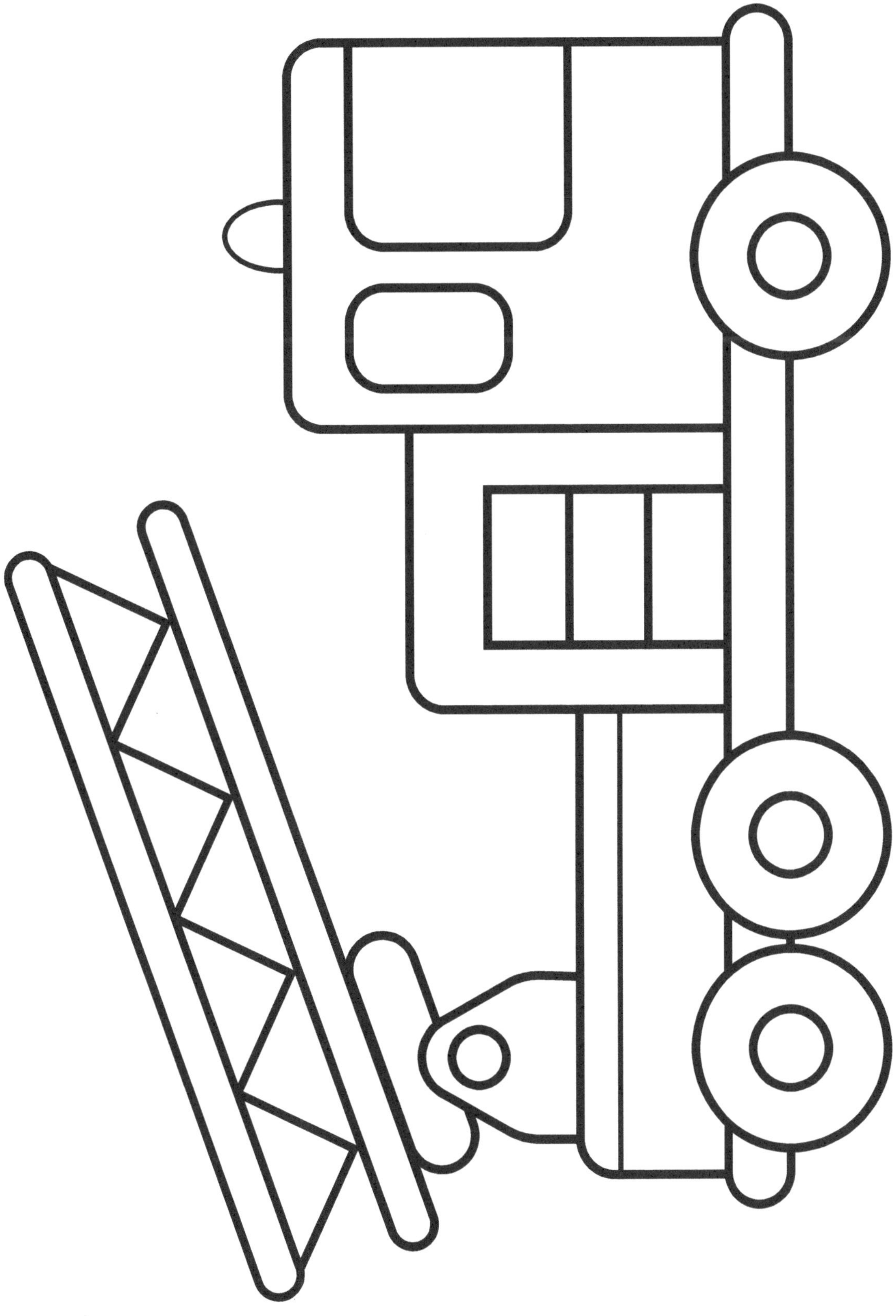

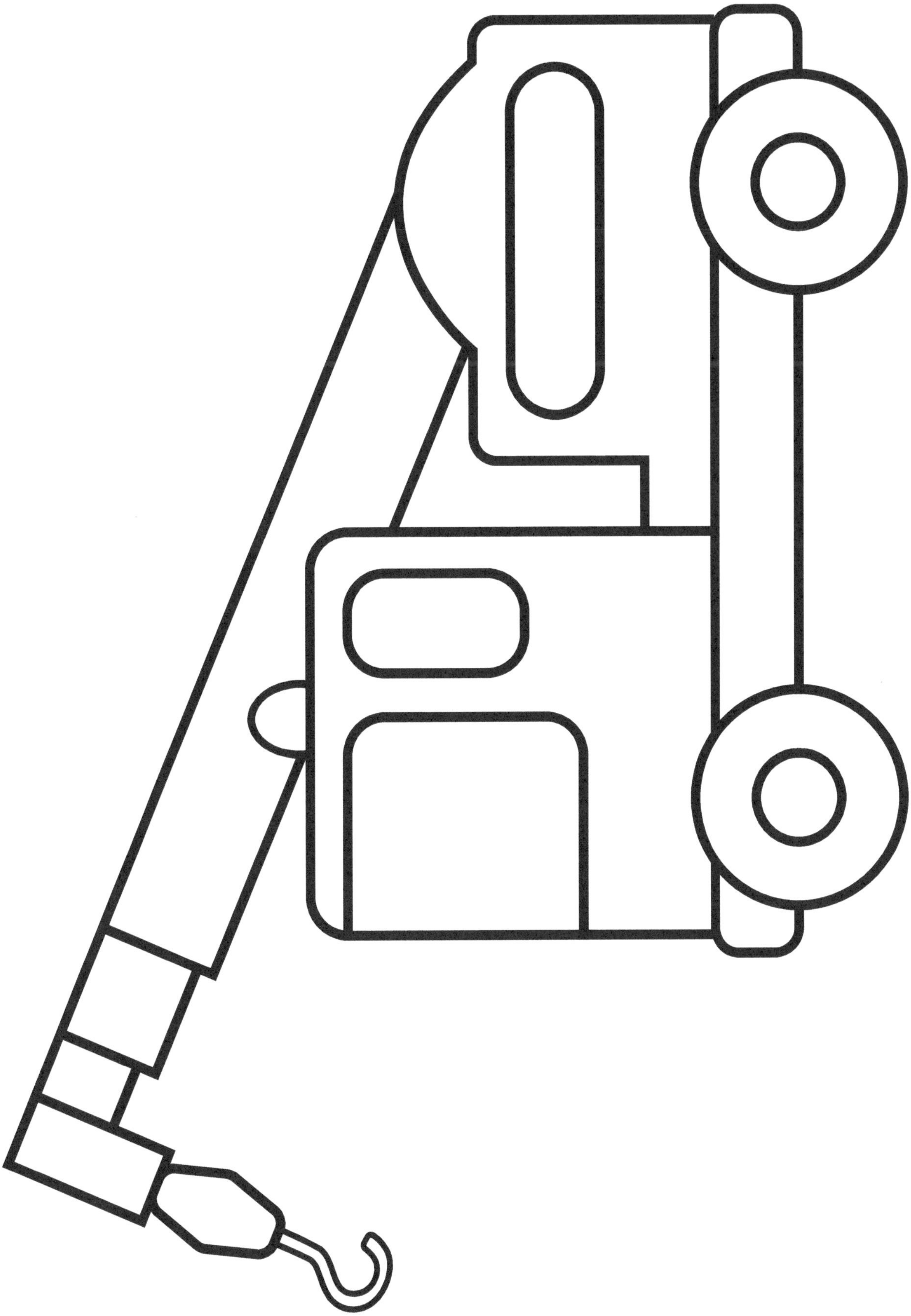

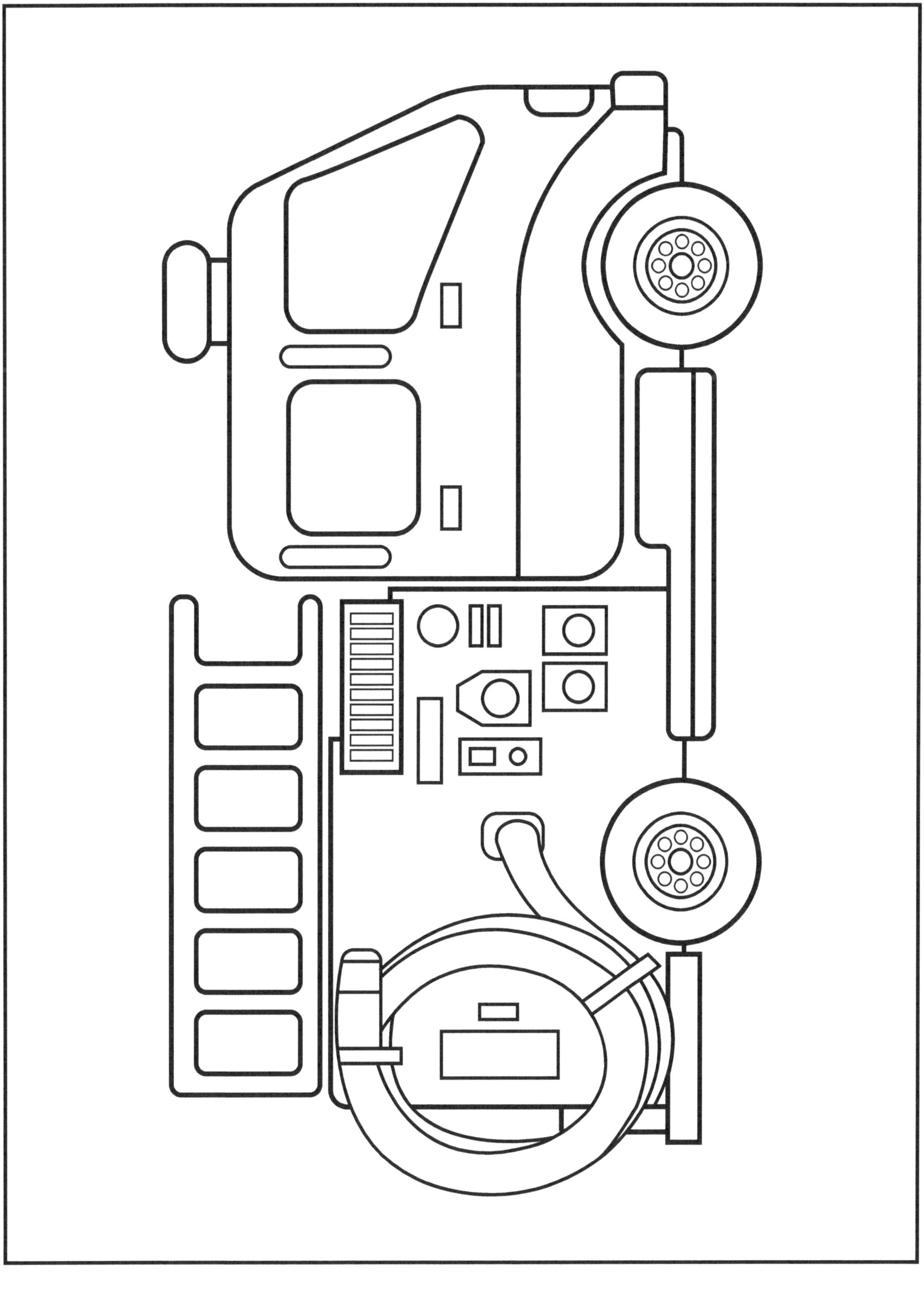

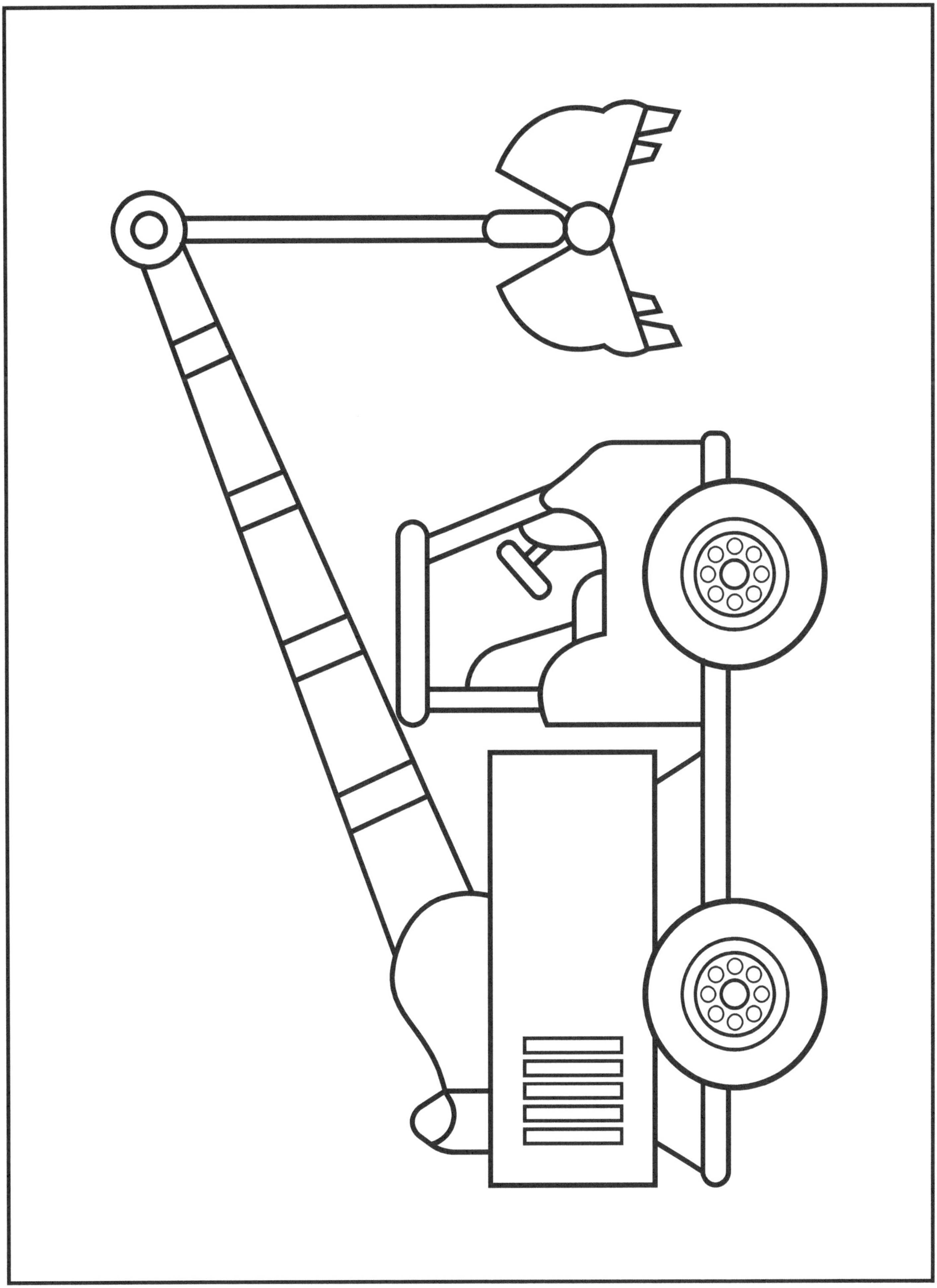

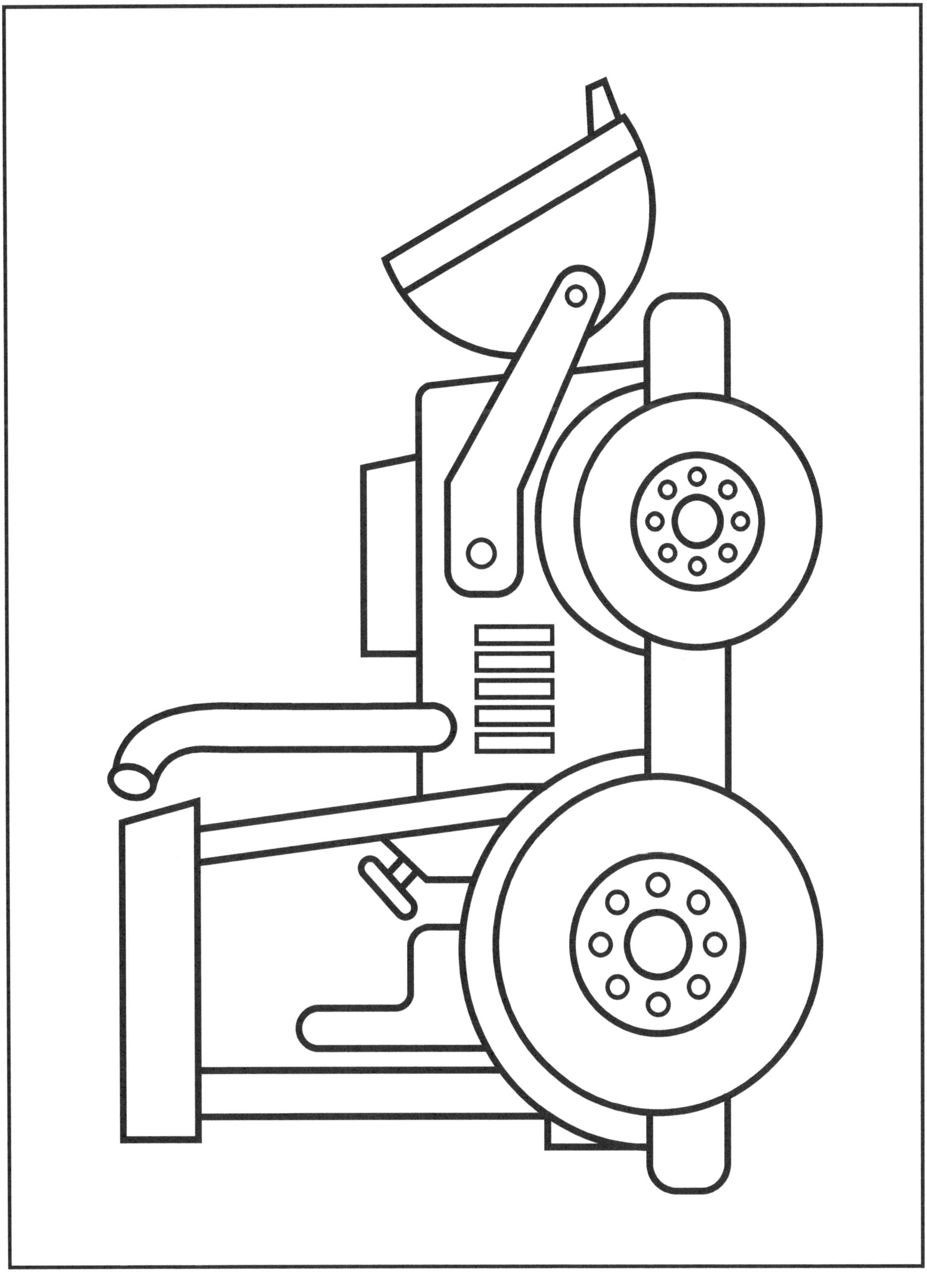

Made in United States
Troutdale, OR
09/17/2024

22882508R10038